FORGIVING

FORGIVING

by

GEORG KÜHLEWIND

ADONIS PRESS
Hawthorne Valley / Harlemville
Ghent, New York

Cover design by Van James

ISBN 0-932776-09-4

THE TRANSLATION

This translation from the original German, based upon that of John Miller and Maria St. Goar, printed in *Journal for Anthroposophy*, Number 33, Spring, 1981, has been revised by Georg Kühlewind, Arvia Ege and the editor.

The reader should note that the English word "cognize" does not fully express the penetrating activity of the German word *"erkennen."* This is undoubtedly connected with its latin origin. *"Erkennen"* gives expression to the living, immediate activity of knowing, of recognizing – the act of perceiving. "Cognize," on the other hand, is a relatively cold, relatively dead word. Hence the translators have combined it with other words in order to approximate more fully the life and quality of "erkennen."

Similarly, the English word *realization*, taken alone, fails to encompass the will element of full accomplishment, the creative activity of bringing something into the realm of reality.

The editor would like to thank the translators as well as Friedemann Schwarzkopf, Christopher Bamford and Erich Boesch for their help and advice.

Christy Barnes, Editor

FORGIVING

Forgive us our trespasses,
as we forgive those who trespass against us.

OUR trespass – our debt – consists of everything that, according to our capabilities, talents and faculties, we could possibly give to others, but which we withhold from them because, out of our very natures, we are obliged, compelled to do this withholding. This gesture of withholding ranges from not-doing – omission – to taking – unjustly; ranges from the passive form of indifference to the aggressive form of hostility and hatred.

This withholding takes place in the realm of life – a realm which, in antithesis to this withholding, knows no allegiance to race, or nation, or to temperament, habit or to any kind of past. In this realm there is no mirrored thinking, no containment. A living form must, however, be contained in order to become the bearer of consciousness. Yet understanding in its inmost nature is truly living, and should in man remain wholly open like the plant, the archetypal plant. This would mean to experience thinking as something living.

Such living thinking, or instantaneous intuition – intuitive knowledge – enables me to recognize what I have caused in another human being and how I have done it, particularly when he has turned against me. In this sense, it is an explicit indication of my own self-knowledge, which I should accept with gratitude. Through this I come to understand why it was necessary for the other to rise up against me, why for me it was necessary to bring him into this situation. All the responsibility rests objectively with me. This recognition of "the reasons" only helps me to recognize where my own weakness lay. This weakness – how did it affect the other, so that he was forced to turn against me? I do not need to "forgive" him; there is nothing there to forgive. Just to understand this and to ask him for forgiveness: this is how I forgive him; this means that my own trespass is forgiven.

The meaning of the plea is "Give us the self-knowledge required to discover our trespass, our guilt towards the other; otherwise it will continue to exist until the time comes when it is discovered." When we really behold the guilt in ourselves, it is forgiven; we no longer have any guilt-feeling. It is not true that the other is to blame. So long as we assume this, we are trapped in our own guilt.

In this way our wrong-doing is forgiven. And as to the wrong-doing of the other, it becomes clear: it was our own.

When the search for fault in ourselves reaches deep enough, we come not only to its immediate and actual cause, but to the basic guilt itself: to the essence of separateness, the core of self-ness, to the not-willing, not-giving, not-yielding, not-forgiving being in us: we come to the one who wants to remain as he is, and so denies us access to the spiritual world.

But this threshold has existed since the original sin. And so the examination of the history of a trespass can lead back to the beginnings. That is the meaning of a trespass. It is for this and because of this that it exists. It is not a question of a knowledge concerning the debts and indebtedness of each human being, but of an experience – the concrete experience of the current indebtedness that can lead to the recognition of the magnitude of our own imperfections.

The Gesture

The spiritual schooling, the concentration, meditation, the exercises which we perform, remain mere maneuvering motions of the ego in the interest of its own existence and strengthening, as long as man does not know the fundamental gesture: the gesture of humility. Until then, the exercising is the ego's preparation for the gesture of self-humbling. But if this gesture, which justifies and sanctifies the exercising, does not occur, it – the process of exercise – remains egotistical. The gesture of humility is the gesture of releasing one's self, of letting oneself fall – a paradoxical gesture, whose power consists of relinquishing the power of the ego (*ich*) so that the existence of the ego is destroyed in the interest of True Being which is unimaginable, neither to be fathomed nor thought up.

As long as I am in the "right" (*Rechthaben*), as long as I hate, as long as I have fear, as long as I live in anxiety, as long as I wait for the other person to begin – just so long can there be no love in me. Love – even if it be only for a single person – drives out all hate, all aversion, every fear. Whenever hate or aversion is in me, or lasting, cultivated anger, my love is of the same substance, is on the same level.

So, too, with my meditation: Light maintains the life of the plant, but the plant brings with it the impurities of the soil.

When I discover: I am *never* right, that truth can never be appropriated, and is therefore no merit of mine, then I can harbor no aversion toward one who has made a mistake, who is "wrong," for it is not his failing.

If, however, I assume that I am right, I should at least draw the only logical conclusion from this view: if the other is in error, makes a mistake, then he is definitely the weaker, the more besieged, the more tempted; I, on the other hand, am the stronger, the healthier one. The potential for helping him is, therefore, mine, and I must initiate the first step. If I wait for him to take the first step, I declare him to be the stronger: I acknowledge that he is in the right. I, however, am caught up in the error.

Whoever seeks or finds the causes, the mistakes, in the other person should immediately look for them in himself; for seeking the error in another was most certainly a sin – a sin of cognition, guilt incurred through the belief in facts, according to which, facts supposedly exist independently of us and of our cognition. Such a fact is supposed to be the fault of another person, a fault which does not concern us, in which we have no part at all. We assume that we have not deprived the other of anything that could have guarded him against making his mistake or error. The cause is "out there" in the other person; his conduct was "such and such." We discover in this attitude – the attitude of naive moral realism – the beginning of the persecution complex! Let us finally realize that it is not the facts that breed fear, aversion, desire or hate, but there are – for me – facts which – in me – "cause" fear, desire, aversion and hate, because fear, aversion, desire, hatred are within me. The facts are such as I am capable of seeing them, of feeling them.

Desire, aversion, fear, anxiety, traditionalism either cling to the past – or flee from it. All these are manifestations of Eros, of the experiencing of myself, and the wanting to experience myself. The sacrifice we are so unwilling to make concretely is the renunciation of what is part of this sphere of experience: the taking offense, the aversion, the vanity. The acceptance of self-humbling is *then* such renunciation no longer, but is now only sincere uprightness, based upon the recognized reality that I am the cause; I am guilty: it is not a matter of waiting for the other to act until. . . . There is no "until"; there is nothing to wait for. This renunciation, once it is done, is feather-light. It is, furthermore, not renunciation, but completion.

All of this applies to him who believes it applies to the other, and also to him who feels it applies to himself.

Whose guilt, then, was not forgiven?

Whom have I not forgiven his guilt?

The gesture is: self-humblement. To admit the unreality of my reasonings, to renounce self-esteem, to abstain from self-gratification on the basis of the facts surrounding the other human being, to let everything fall away – including myself – and also to relinquish any pride in this act: this is the white magic which finds its beginning and end in the undoing of the spell and in the transformation of my own being. Nothing else is required. The world and my fellow man must only be *seen* in their reality; *here* lies the root of the spell of enchantment with regard to the world. White magic consists in man's making the path clear for what must happen, that he not protest, not resist. Then it also occurs. The occurrence is not human doing.

One must not weigh the consequences of the gesture. You cannot weigh them anyway, because what follows is no human occurrence. When you consider and weigh, you are not doing anything in any case.

He is great who is able to humble himself, and who also does not take pride in this, his greatness – who is not humble out of arrogance.

He who does not wish to conquer is unconquerable.

Let yourself drop away.

Illness is not lack of strength, but a sign of sensitivity. Out of it, strengths are born. He who does not realize that he is ill is not therefore well. He who does not recognize that *he* has made the mistake has certainly made it, and, more than that, doubles it.

Love your enemy. He provides a reason for the humbling of yourself, for the recognition of your own reality. He offers you the opportunity not to be hostile, to love your enemy. He has accepted the role of the weaker, so that you could give up your obstinate conviction that you are right, your self-pride, your self – so that there should be someone whom you do not wish to conquer, over whom you do not wish to be king, since you have recognized as a true fact your own solitary kingship which rules over not one single subject. Love your enemy, for he is not your enemy: He is that only if you consider him to be so.

Being good and forgiving shall not be the goals of your striving: all that is pride and arrogance; let your striving be only to cognize – to recognize the true; that suffices. It is enough if you cognize: what you experience as your most precious Self is actually a disturbance in world existence. Ask to be forgiven for existing.

Love is only love if there within it disavowal, misunderstanding, rejection, resistance, have already been encompassed. The new commandment is: Love one another, as I have loved you. It is the forgiveness of betrayal, of faithlessness, even before it is committed. Such "embrace" creates you and sustains you even now.

*Realization**

Whoever views the foregoing as rules, or advice, and consequently strives to realize it, has misunderstood it. What has thus been described can only be realized by one who cognizes it — who recognizes it. True cognizing — "knowing" — is not acknowledgment, not acceptance of what has been communicated. It is not discernment either, but intensified meditation. It is not a matter of norms or standards but of the formulation of meditations that can only be followed by a further meditation. Instantaneous cognition — not a previously acquired view, even if beheld in intensified cognition — is always required for the realization, the "making real," the making actual of something. For true realization, memory does not suffice.

He who truly cognizes a communication in its own immediate situation gains, together with this cognition, the strength and the potential for

---

*See note on translation, p. v.

realization as actual accomplishment. He gains intuition for the concrete event and the power with which the intuition can be brought forth from the depths of his own being acting here upon earth. With this he takes a step toward the realization of true self-awareness: the synthesis of the long-separated powers of cognizing – of knowing – and of willing.

He who approaches the foregoing thus *cognitively,* receives the powers of realization – of accomplishing something in the realm of reality. As long as they were bound to his egohood, it was these very powers that hindered cognition. Cognition is surrender – devotion. The forces of surrender are used by the soul, in its ego-existence, in connection with and in the use of the body. Cognizing and morality, on the other hand, are fed and sustained by just these same forces. They stream out in the direction of surrender either to the body or to the world. So all the efforts of mirrored consciousness are of no avail: no morality is born from it, for its creative powers are surrendered to the body. It is just for this reason that it is mirrored consciousness.

In meditative consciousness, however, we must

experience the becoming-with, the transformation "into" what is cognized. There *is* no other way. It is self-surrender, self-extinguishing – pain. It is joy: the coming-into-being in the *other* – realization, accomplishment. The metamorphosis is: cognition. Cognition – intuitive knowing – is metamorphosis. Only that cognition which takes place upon the mirrored surface has separated itself from true Being, in order that it may gain understanding of Being and of itself. The greatest hinderance to realization is the *fact*. Fact, however, is always an already-cognized fact. Just as the already-seen is not the cause of seeing, so the fact also does not cause me to cognize it. Just as the already-seen is the result of seeing, so also is the fact the result of my cognition, and is my experience. And it goes without saying that this experience is never completed as long as I live. Therefore the face of the fact can change, and does change in most cases during life. Today's misfortune can prove to be a blessing; the joy of today can prove to be a tragic error. The one for whom the facts do not change or develop can well suspect that he is not on the right path. Facts gradually turn out to be what they really are.

They have no final face for us, they live with us: as long as we live, they only begin. The facts have not occurred: they occur constantly.

The facts always tell us something, mostly in inverted language, for we do not understand their true language. If we did comprehend it, perhaps much would take a different course. But according to how we understand the language, it superimposes itself upon our feeling-life. The true language of facts is the original, higher language of our deeper feeling nature which, however, we resist with every nerve and fiber of our body. The facts are planned and carried out by our true Self, and therefore we pit ourselves against this with all our might.

Whoever believes the facts to be outer occurrences turns the world just as upside down as the one who believes he knows that there is a world that is quite independent of his cognition. Once cognition meant change, reshaping, transformation. Teaching signified transformation because the powers of cognition were then cosmic powers, powers of being. In the early stage of the formation of mirrored consciousness, moral commandments could still be effective. A morality which was developed from outward sources was still possible. Still earlier, the sensory organs and the organs of cognition were simultaneously formative organs. Comprehension and self-formation were one and the same process. There was no without, no within, there was only world-process. Still earlier, there was no female, no male; only the *human being*.

Consciousness of self, the awareness of the true "I," is the synthesis of the powers of cognizing and the powers of willing, in which there is no inner and outer, no man and woman. The power of synthesis comes into motion in love – the highest power of world consciousness, a power standing above man and woman – which helps a new "I"-bearer into its earthly existence. It is only the true "I" that can accomplish this. Its power is active in man and woman alike, in the *human being*. Today, this power of self-awareness is still sleeping, dreaming. Yet it must also bestir itself in the actualization, in the real-ization of forgiveness, of humility. Because it is still sleeping, dreaming, it can be directly moved only in intensified cognition. The world process is a single process, outwardly as well as inwardly. *World* is the world, cognition and man in one, a single process: cognizing. The world is: *cognizing* – knowing in its true living reality. For this reason, wonder is the true starting point of cognition. I discover that which I do not yet understand – and yet, at the same time, I behold it. Wonder originates within the world process; it belongs to this, not to the facts; it leads towards that whence it sprang.

It is advisable to accept wonder and astonishment, with devotion and surrender, what the facts – and most especially the hostile facts – offer me, as I accept everything that the world offers. And so, accepting their lesson – not with resistance, but positively, that is through intuition – I can, without prejudice – in non-imitative, brand-new, unpreconceived cognition – allow the facts to reveal to me what they want to teach me. What they teach is acceptance. Acceptance, however, means: I must understand what I am supposed to accept, otherwise I do not accept *that*. *That* becomes through my cognition. The redemption has already taken place, otherwise we would not resist it. The capacities and methods for its attainment stand at man's disposal: the World in its own light.

Real-ization is acceptance; acceptance – cognition; cognition – transformation. "*Beloved, now we are the sons of God, and it doth not yet appear what we shall be; but we know that, when He shall appear, we shall be like Him; for we shall see Him as He is*" (1 John 3:2).